The European Union
Political, Social, and Economic Cooperation

THE EUROPEAN UNION
FACT & FIGURES

by
James Stafford

Mason Crest Publishers
Philadelphia

Mason Crest Publishers Inc.
370 Reed Road, Broomall, Pennsylvania 19008
(866) MCP-BOOK (toll free)
www.masoncrest.com

13 12 11 10 09 08 07   10 9 8 7 6 5 4 3 2

Library of Congress Cataloging-in-Publication Data

Stafford, James, 1963-
    The European Union : facts and figures / by James Stafford.
        p. cm. — (The European Union)
    Includes bibliographical references and index.
        ISBN 1-4222-0045-0
        ISBN 1-4222-0038-8 (series)
    1. European Union. 2. European Union countries—Economic integration. 3. Regionalism—European Union countries. I. Title. II. European Union (Series) (Philadelphia, Pa.)
        JN30.S72 2006
        341.242'2—dc22
                            2005018272

Produced by Harding House Publishing Service, Inc.
www.hardinghousepages.com
Interior design by Benjamin Stewart.
Cover design by MK Bassett-Harvey.
Printed in the Hashemite Kingdom of Jordan.

Contents

THE
EUROPEAN
UNION
Established in 1950

ICELAND

GREENLAND
SEA

BARENTS
SEA

NORWEGIAN
SEA

RUSSIA

White
Sea

FINLAND

NORWAY

SWEDEN

DENMARK

UNITED KINGDOM

IRELAND

NORTH SEA

BALTIC
SEA

RUSSIA

ESTONIA

LATVIA

LITHUANIA

BELARUS

POLAND

THE NETHERLANDS

BELGIUM
LUXEMBOURG

GERMANY

CZECH REPUBLIC

SLOVAKIA

UKRAINE

MOLDOVA

FRANCE

SWITZERLAND

AUSTRIA

HUNGARY

SLOVENIA

ROMANIA

BLACK
SEA

PORTUGAL

SPAIN

ITALY

BOSNIA-
HERCEGOVINA
CROATIA

YUGOSLAVIA

MACEDONIA

ALBANIA

BULGARIA

TURKEY

CYPRUS

SYRIA

LEBANON

GREECE

MEDITERRANEAN SEA

MALTA

MEDITERRANEAN SEA

MOROCCO

ALGERIA

TUNISIA

LIBYA

EGYPT

JORDAN

ISRAEL &
THE PALESTINIAN
TERRITORIES

INTRODUCTION

Sixty years ago, Europe lay scarred from the battles of the Second World War. During the next several years, a plan began to take shape that would unite the countries of the European continent so that future wars would be inconceivable. On May 9, 1950, French Foreign Minister Robert Schuman issued a declaration calling on France, Germany, and other European countries to pool together their coal and steel production as "the first concrete foundation of a European federation." "Europe Day" is celebrated each year on May 9 to commemorate the beginning of the European Union (EU).

The EU consists of twenty-five countries, spanning the continent from Ireland in the west to the border of Russia in the east. Eight of the ten most recently admitted EU member states are former communist regimes that were behind the Iron Curtain for most of the latter half of the twentieth century.

Any European country with a democratic government, a functioning market economy, respect for fundamental rights, and a government capable of implementing EU laws and policies may apply for membership. Bulgaria and Romania are set to join the EU in 2007. Croatia and Turkey have also embarked on the road to EU membership.

While the EU began as an idea to ensure peace in Europe through interconnected economies, it has evolved into so much more today:

- Citizens can travel freely throughout most of the EU without carrying a passport and without stopping for border checks.

- EU citizens can live, work, study, and retire in another EU country if they wish.

- The euro, the single currency accepted throughout twelve of the EU countries (with more to come), is one of the EU's most tangible achievements, facilitating commerce and making possible a single financial market that benefits both individuals and businesses.

- The EU ensures cooperation in the fight against cross-border crime and terrorism.

- The EU is spearheading world efforts to preserve the environment.

- As the world's largest trading bloc, the EU uses its influence to promote fair rules for world trade, ensuring that globalization also benefits the poorest countries.

- The EU is already the world's largest donor of humanitarian aid and development assistance, providing 55 percent of global official development assistance to developing countries in 2004.

The EU is neither a nation intended to replace existing nations, nor an international organization. The EU is unique—its member countries have established common institutions to which they delegate some of their sovereignty so that decisions on matters of joint interest can be made democratically at the European level.

Europe is a continent with many different traditions and languages, but with shared values such as democracy, freedom, and social justice, cherished values well known to North Americans. Indeed, the EU motto is "United in Diversity."

Enjoy your reading. Take advantage of this chance to learn more about Europe and the EU!

Ambassador John Bruton,
Head of Delegation of the European Commission, Washington, D.C.

London is a major European business center.

1 The Historic Path to the European Union

By the beginning of the twentieth century, the people of Europe had grown tired of the constant wars between its various countries. Hopes rose for a union that would allow the citizens of Europe to trade with one another, travel, and support each other's interests. These hopes were

The formation of the EU was the beginning of a new day for Europe.

postponed by two great wars during the first half of the twentieth century—World War I (1914–1919) and World War II (1939–1945). However, by mid-twentieth century, those people who had resisted the forces of hatred and dictatorship within these wars, worked even harder to create a union of European nations that could live in peaceful cooperation. World leaders who supported the new European order included Konrad Adenauer of Germany, Winston Churchill of England, and Robert Schuman of France.

During this period, Robert Schuman, France's foreign affairs minister, put into practice an idea originally proposed by Jean Monnet: to set up a European Coal and Steel Community, known as the ECSC. The ECSC was officially created by the

Treaty of Paris in 1951, and established a **common market** in coal and steel. Having a common market meant that steps had been taken to allow various countries within Europe to do business with one another more easily. Sharing the new common market healed some of the hard feelings between the countries that had just been at war with each other, and it led businesses toward the peaceful uses of the materials that had previously been used for war.

The ECSC was the first step in the process that led to the European Union (EU) of today. In fact, the ECSC's goal has been largely achieved today—goods move freely across borders, with little paperwork and few if any customs duties (the fees that are paid when goods travel between countries).

Historic steps led to the EU's formation.

Quick Facts: The European Union

Number of Member Countries: 25

Official Languages: 20—Czech, Danish, Dutch, English, Estonian, Finnish, French, German, Greek, Hungarian, Italian, Latvian, Lithuanian, Maltese, Polish, Portuguese, Slovak, Slovenian, Spanish, and Swedish; additional language for treaty purposes: Irish Gaelic.

Motto: *In Varietate Concordia* (United in Diversity)

European Council's President: Each member state takes a turn to lead the council's activities for 6 months.

European Commission's President: José Manuel Barroso (Portugal)

European Parliament's President: Josep Borrell (Spain)

Total Area: 1,502,966 square miles (3,892,685 sq. km.)

Population: 454,900,000

Population Density: 302.7 people/square mile (116.8 people/sq. km.)

GDP: €9.61.1012

Per Capita GDP: €21,125

Formation:
- Declared: February 7, 1992, with signing of the Maastricht Treaty
- Recognized: November 1, 1993, with the ratification of the Maastricht Treaty

Community Currency: Euro. Currently 12 of the 25 member states have adopted the euro as their currency.

Anthem: "Ode to Joy"

Flag: Blue background with 12 gold stars arranged in a circle

Official Day: Europe Day, May 9.

Source: europa.eu.int

In 1957, The Treaty of Rome set up the European Economic Community, the EEC. The goals of the EEC went further than ECSC's goals for free trade. These new, more ambitious goals included social progress, economic improvement, and the continual improvement of social and living conditions. The EEC originally had six member countries: Belgium, France, Germany, Italy, Luxembourg, and the Netherlands. Over the years, the EEC evolved into today's EU.

The EU has always been open to states that are able to take on its economic challenges and implement its rules. For example, EU member states must agree to abide by a customs union, a single market, and an economic and monetary union.

Common policies for all the member states, mostly for trade and agriculture, were first set up during the 1960s, and customs duties were removed on July 1, 1968. All these economic and social policies worked so well that Denmark, Ireland, and the United Kingdom decid-

The EU opens the door to new opportunities for its member nations.

CHAPTER ONE—THE HISTORIC PATH TO THE EUROPEAN UNION

The EU provides practical means for achieving new goals.

ed to join the EU in 1973, bringing the total number of member states to nine. At that time, the EU also began to take on even more tasks, including new social, regional, and environmental policies. To put these policies into practice, the European Regional Development Fund (ERDF) was set up in 1975.

Also, in the early 1970s the EU realized it needed a monetary union. At the same time though, the United States decided to suspend the dollar's compatibility into gold. The United States' decision caused a period of great instability on the world's money markets. Such instability was then worsened by the oil crises of 1973 and 1979.

Finally, the European Monetary System (EMS) began in 1979 and helped stabilize currency exchange rates between European countries and the rest of the world. The EMS encouraged EU member states to pass their own strict policies within their own countries, while also sharing power with each other.

In 1981, Greece joined the EU, followed by Spain and Portugal in 1986. These new entries made it urgent to introduce structural programs, such as the first Integrated Mediterranean Programmes (IMP), aimed at reducing the economic gaps between the richest and poorest member states.

During the 1970s and 1980s, the EU began to play a more prominent role outside of Europe. Between 1975 and 1989, the EU signed a series of **conventions** with African countries and island nations of the Caribbean and the Pacific. Known as Lome I, II, III, and IV, the conventions focused on aid and trade policies. These conventions eventually led to the Cotonou Agreement of

> The EU works toward peace.

June 2000, which has the goal of creating a common foreign and security policy for these countries.

The worldwide recession during the early 1980s caused great concern in Europe, but in 1985 Jacques Delors, the president of the Economic Commission of the European Union, published a "White Paper" setting a timetable for completing the European Single Market by January 1, 1993. The European Single Market would break down many of the divisions between the countries' economies, allowing them to trade as if they were all part of one large economic system. The policies suggested within Delors' White Paper became known as the Single European Act and were signed in February 1986. The act became official on July 1, 1987.

In Maastricht, in the Netherlands, on December 1991, the Treaty on European Union was passed and became officially recognized on November 1, 1993. Within this treaty, institutions were given greater responsibilities, and the EU as it is known today was created. At that time, the EEC was renamed the European Community. Original goals included the creation of a monetary union by 1999, European citizenship, and new common policies, including a European foreign and security policy. When Austria, Finland, and Sweden joined on January 1, 1995, there were now fifteen members. Twelve of these countries replaced their currencies with the euro on January 1, 2002, a currency that today has a similar status to the U.S. dollar.

In Lisbon, Portugal, March 2000, a meeting took place to discuss strategies for modernizing

Cyprus joined the EU in 2004.

Europe's economy so that the countries of Europe could better compete in the world market. The Lisbon Strategy, which came from this meeting, opened up all sectors to competition, encouraging innovation and business investment, and modernizing Europe's education systems to meet the needs of an **information society**.

Almost as soon as the EU grew to fifteen members, another twelve asked to be admitted. In the mid-1990s, applications came from Soviet bloc Bulgaria, Czech Republic, Hungary, Poland, Romania, and Slovakia.

After the fall of communism in 1990, the EU supported **democratization** in former communist countries, giving them technical and financial assistance as they introduced **market economies**. Following this aid, three Baltic states that had been part of the Soviet Union (Estonia, Latvia, Lithuania), one republic of the former Yugoslavia (Slovenia), and two Mediterranean countries (Cypress and Malta) requested admittance into the EU.

For ten of these twelve candidate countries, the negotiations were complete on December 13, 2002, in Copenhagen. By 2004, the EU increased its membership five times, and had expanded to twenty-five member states. The enlargement in 2004 brought in eight countries from central and Eastern Europe, and the Mediterranean islands of Malta and Cyprus. With the 450 million people of its twenty-five member states, the EU has more citizens than the combined populations of the United States and Russia. However, the ten new countries are poorer than the EU average, so raising their standards of living is a new priority for all the member states. Two other countries, Bulgaria and Romania, expect to become members in 2007. Turkey is the thirteenth country with hopes of someday becoming an EU member state.

In the last fifty years, the EU has become the world's second-largest economy, with twelve countries sharing a single currency. It is a growing political force in world events, and its size and importance will likely continue to grow in the twenty-first century.

Tourists to Portofino enjoy the traveling convenience provided by Italy's membership in the EU.

2 CHAPTER HOW THE EUROPEAN UNION WORKS

Unlike the United States, the EU is not a **federation**. And unlike the United Nations, it is not simply a method of cooperation between governments. Instead, member states of the EU keep their own self-governments, at the same time that they allow European institutions to make some of their decisions.

The three decision-making bodies that create the laws within the entire EU are the European Parliament—which is elected democratically by European citizens—the Council of the European Union—whose members represent individual member states—and the European Commission—which represents the entire EU. Rules for these institutions begin in treaties, which are agreed on by the various branches of government within each of the member states.

Treaties are amended each time new member states join, which is usually every decade or so. Treaties have allowed the EEC to gradually take on more and more social, environmental, and regional policies. For example, the Treaty of Maastricht introduced two new areas of cooperation between the member states: defense and justice. The Treaty of Maastricht also renamed the EEC the European Community.

Other important treaties include the Single European Act (SEA), which was ratified in February 1986 and established by July 1987. This act prepared the countries of the EU to trade with each other within a single market economy. The Treaty of Amsterdam was signed on October 2, 1997, and became effective on May 1, 1999. This treaty amended other EU and European Community treaties. Finally, the Treaty of Nice was signed on February 26, 2001, and was implemented on February 1, 2003. This treaty amended the other treaties in order to allow other countries to join the EU more easily.

Treaties also provide the rules for European decision making. There are three main methods for enacting laws. In police and judicial matters, to revise treaties, and to alter economic policy, parliament must provide its opinion, or **consultation**. In jobs of the European Central Bank,

The flags of the EU's nations:

top row, left to right
Belgium, the Czech Republic, Denmark, Germany, Estonia, Greece

second row, left to right
Spain, France, Ireland, Italy, Cyprus, Latvia

third row, left to right
Lithuania, Luxembourg, Hungary, Malta, the Netherlands, Austria

bottom row, left to right
Poland, Portugal, Slovenia, Slovakia, Finland, Sweden, United Kingdom

The European Parliament's offices in Luxembourg

certain international agreements, and to accept new member states, the European Council has to attain parliament's **assent**. In regard to the environment, education, and employment, parliament shares power with the Council of the European Union by **co-decision**.

The European Parliament has monthly sessions in Strasbourg, France, which is the parliament's seat. Within the European Parliament, the Parliamentary Committee meetings are in Brussels, Belgium. Luxembourg is the home of the administrative offices of the European Parliament.

The European Parliament shares with the European Council the power to make laws. It supervises the EU institutions, in particular, the European Commission. It can reject nominations of the commission, and has the right to **censure** the commission as a whole. It shares with the council authority over the EU budget.

The Council of the European Union is the **legislative** arm of the union, with one minister from each country, and a rotation of those ministers every six months. The council meets in Brussels, Belgium, except for April, June, and October when meetings are in Luxembourg. Which members attend a particular meeting depends on the issues under discussion at that meeting. Committees that make up the council include:

- General Affairs and External Relations

- Economic and Financial Affairs

- Employment

- Social Policy

- Health and Consumer Affairs

- Competitiveness

- Transport, Telecommunications, and Energy

- Agriculture and Fisheries

- Environment

- Education

- Youth and Culture

Past and Future Presidents of the Council:

2003	First half year:	Greece
	Second half:	Italy
2004	First half year:	Ireland
	Second half:	Netherlands
2005	First half year:	Luxembourg
	Second half:	United Kingdom
2006	First half year:	Austria
	Second half:	Finland

The council has six main responsibilities:

1. It passes laws, often jointly, with European Parliament.

2. It coordinates broad economic policies of EU members.

3. It concludes international agreements between the EU and one or more states.

4. It approves the budget of the European Parliament.

5. It develops the EU's common foreign and security policy.

6. It **mediates** between national courts and police in criminal matters.

In January 2003, for example, the European Union Police Mission began operations in Bosnia and Herzegovina, taking over the civilian aspects of crisis management from UN Peacekeepers. To enable the EU to respond more effectively to international crises, the European Council decided at the Helsinki Summit meeting in December 1999 that the union would create a "Rapid Rotation Force" of up to 60,000 military personnel that could be **deployed** within sixty days and be kept in operation for a least a year.

An example of the work of the Justice of Home Affairs, one of the council's individual committees, is its work on the problems of drugs, terrorism, international fraud, trafficking in human beings, and the sexual exploitation of children. Such work is a c c o m p l i s h e d because of cooperation between EU member states.

In Brussels, each member state has a permanent representative, called an ambassador, to the European Council. Ambassadors meet weekly to prepare the work of the council. The presidency of the council rotates every six months.

Number of votes cast by the various member states:

Germany: 29
France: 29
Italy: 29
United Kingdom: 29
Spain: 27
Poland: 27
Netherlands: 13
Belgium: 12
Czech Republic: 12
Greece: 12
Hungary: 12
Portugal: 12
Austria: 10
Sweden: 10
Denmark: 7
Ireland: 7
Lithuania: 7
Slovakia: 7
Finland: 7
Cyprus: 4
Estonia: 4
Latvia: 4
Luxembourg: 4
Slovenia: 4
Malta: 3

The council's president is aided by the General Secretariat. Decisions in council are decided by vote, with the number of votes cast by each country representing its population in comparison to the populations of the other countries.

The European Commission suggests legislation and implements decisions made by the parliament and the council. Together, the governments within the EU agree on a president. The president and members of the states choose nineteen other members of the European Commission. The parliament then interviews and approves the nominees.

There are 24,000 officials, experts, and translators who do the work of the European Commission at its seat, which is in Brussels, Belgium. The commission's main duties include proposing legislation to parliament and council, managing and implementing EU policies and its budget, enforcing European law with the Court of Justice, and representing the EU on the world stage. The European Commission proposes action only if it believes national, regional, or local interests can't solve a problem. This is called the "subsidiary principle."

The Court of Justice makes legal judgments on cases brought before it. There is one judge from each EU member state, with eight advocates general. The advocates assist judges and present reasoned opinions. Members of both courts are appointed for renewable terms of six years.

Common cases heard by the courts include requests for a preliminary ruling. This helps various EU member states to interpret laws the same way. There are also "proceedings for failure to fulfill an

The Court of Justice

obligation," when any member of the EU fails to keep a promise. And there are also proceedings for "annulment," when a claim is made that a law is illegal, as well as "failures to act," when European Parliament or the European Commission fail to take a required action.

Apart from institutions, there are also nineteen agencies within the EU. Agencies differ from institutions in that they are not provided for by treaties, but rather, have been created by individual pieces of legislation and are set up to perform specific tasks. The European Court of **Auditors** is independent of the other institutions and checks that EU funds are used properly. There is one auditor from each country handling EU income or expenditure. The European Central Bank was set up in 1998. It manages the euro within the twelve countries that have now adopted the euro for currency. Its main job is keeping **inflation** under control. The European Economic and Social Committee represents civil society—such as trade unions, farmers, and consumers. The Committee of the Regions represents regional and local authorities with respect to issues like the environment, education, or transportation. The European Investment Bank finances EU projects. Last of all, the European Ombudsman uncovers **maladministration** of the EU. It is an **intermediary** between citizens and the EU, looking at complaints from citizens of the member states.

Wind power is vital to the EU's energy economy.

3 THE EUROPEAN UNION AND EUROPE'S ECONOMY

In 1957, the Treaty of Rome established what was then the EEC and what is today the EU. When this community began, the goods moving within its borders from country to country had to pay customs duties. Today, almost fifty years later, the EU is considered a single economy.

In 1969, the EU set itself the objective of achieving economic and monetary union by 1980. Going beyond the goals it has set for itself, in the past fifty years the EU has become the world's second-largest economy, with twelve countries sharing a single currency. Its goods move freely between countries, as do service providers such as airlines, banks, and phone companies.

The makeup of the European economy has changed greatly during the past five decades. In 1958, 23 percent of the population in the six countries of the EEC relied on farming for a job. By 2001, less than 4 percent of the then-fifteen members of the EU, relied on farming. On the other hand, in 1958, 40 percent worked in industry; this percentage dropped to 29 percent in 2001. Today, *service industries* are the largest source of jobs, with 67 percent of the EU's population working in these jobs in 2001, compared to 37 percent in 1958.

Three key steps to breaking down barriers to trade within the EU have been:

1. The creation of a customs union—which began the process of free trade.

2. The establishment of a single market—which eliminated much of the paperwork involved with trade.

3. The economic and monetary union—which removed barriers to cross-border investment.

When the Customs Union was completed in 1968, free trade quickly opened up in the EU. Businesses from Lapland to Sicily, from Portugal's Atlantic Islands to the EU's easternmost borders no longer paid customs duties. The Customs Union also **standardized** duties on imports that arrived from various parts of the world. Importers to the EU have now begun bringing shipments in bulk, and then breaking them down for delivery to various member states.

Because of the Customs Union, by 1970, member states were trading six times as much between themselves than they were twelve years earlier. They were also trading three times as much with the rest of the world. Their economies doubled in size and expanded faster than the U.S. economy.

After the successes of the Customs Union, some obstacles still remained, particularly in developing common EU standards for issues such as environmental regulations and technical requirements. The SEA, with its plans for the European Single Market, was signed in 1986 1992 as the target date for eliminatin the remaining trade barriers in the EU. Single Market in place took more th

The EU's united economy has allowed it to become a worldwide financial power.

sand pieces of legislation in seven years. It eased checks on goods as they crossed borders, and it allowed countries to trust one another's standards and technologies. Competition was then intro-duced into areas traditionally held by ***monopolies***, such as telecommunications, airlines, the railways, postal services, gas, and electricity.

© BCE ECB EZB EKT EKP 2002

© BCE ECB EZB EKT EKP 2002

© BCE ECB EZB EKT EKP 2002

© BCE ECB EZB EKT EKP 2002

© BCE ECB EZB EKT EKP 2002

The euro, the EU's currency

Between 1992 and 2002, the EU's Single Market has:

1. generated 900 billion euros in extra prosperity—which amounts to almost 6,000 euros per household.

2. contributed to a 30 percent increase in manufactured goods.

3. been a key factor in boosting investment with the EU twelvefold.

4. made the EU internationally competitive

5. allocated skills efficiently, by giving workers the choice to work with various countries.

6. boosted purchasing power by putting pressure on prices.

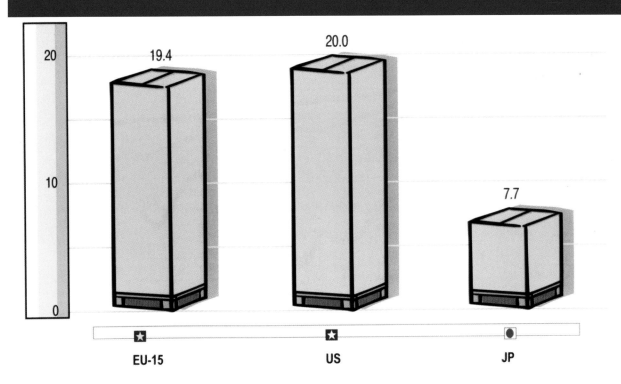

The EU's share of the world's total trade in goods in 2001, compared with the United States and Japan

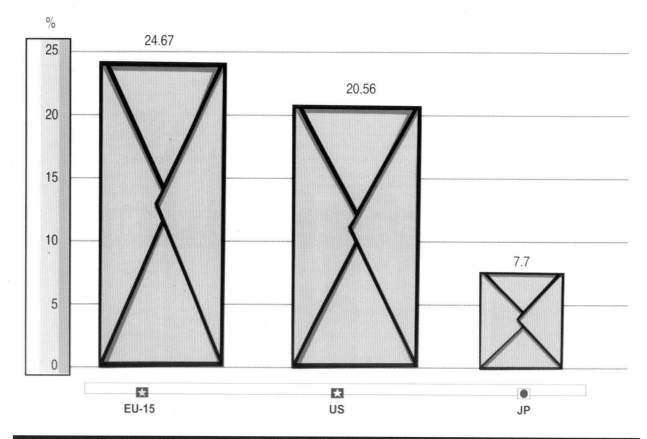

%

25		
20		
15		
10		
5		
0		

24.67

20.56

7.7

⭐
EU-15

⭐
US

●
JP

The EU's share of the world's total trade in services in 2001, compared with the United States and Japan

Part of the advantage of the Single Market economy has been the introduction of the euro. The standardization of the euro within the EU ensures a low inflation environment, and it gives European countries an international currency with which to deal with the rest of the world.

Euro notes and coins were introduced on January 1, 2002—seven different notes and eight different coins. Each coin has a euro design on one side and a symbol of its specific country on the other. Unlike the coins, euro notes are standard from country to country. Before these coins and notes were introduced, Europeans were burdened by the costs of changing their money as they trav-

Million

120
110
100
90
80
70
60
50
40
30
20
10
0

44.1   44.3

8.0   7.1

1995   2001
Agriculture

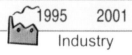
1995   2001
Industry

116.4

102.9

1995   2001

Services

eled from country to country. Today, however, people can shop more efficiently, even comparing prices for goods as those prices differ from country to country.

Another hurdle to overcome within the Single Market was the continual enlargement of the EU. Initial costs of expansion are high as the EU helps newcomers complete the transition to becoming free-market economies. However, all member states benefit since competition and increased personal mobility are good for growth. Also, newcomers expect 1 percent more growth each year from membership. Standards of living and quality of life are improving, and 300,000 new jobs are projected for those countries by 2010.

In 1990, the EU lifted its last remaining restrictions on taking money from one member state to another. Because of these lifted restrictions, governments were no longer able to turn to central banks to print money to bail them out if they could not balance their budgets. In 1994, the European Monetary Institute was formed, the forerunner of today's European Central Bank (ECB). EU member states now agree on a system of "multilateral surveillance" to watch places where one member state's decisions might have adverse effects on the economies of the others.

The Stability and Growth Pact commits all EU member states to the principle of budgets that are at least *nearly* balanced. This pact keeps governments from increasing taxes, and it also frees governments to spend money on its citizens, rather than on debt repayments. If economic growth does slow within a country, some borrowing may be justified; however, the Stability and Growth Pact

ensures that an excessive **deficit** in one EU country does not have negative effects on the others.

The ECB plays a crucial role in achieving stability for the euro area. It does so by setting the interest rates it uses in its dealings with banks, which in turn act as a baseline for all euro-area interest rates. The bank also manages the currency reserves of all the euro area, and has the power to sell and buy foreign exchange on international currency markets.

When the euro was introduced in 1999, European governments were in most cases immediately paying less interest on money they borrowed. A low inflation environment, in a market where there were plenty of buyers and sellers, also aids the governments. Lower interest rates keep the cost of debt repayment down and leave governments more money to spend on health, pensions, social welfare, or the inner workings of their governments.

Competition and room to expand in the single market helps keep European companies leaders of the world. Of the world's one hundred largest companies, thirty-two are from the EU. So are thirty-nine of the world's one hundred largest commercial banks and twenty-seven of the one hundred most valuable brands.

Not only do member states benefit from the EU's new economy, but many other countries throughout the world benefit as well. Many countries are now borrowing in the euro because it is an internationally recognized currency. Also, the euro gives countries another option to diversify their holdings. Today, the euro is increasingly competitive with the U.S. dollar for use by banks as reserve currency (currency kept for monetary crises).

Cyprus, one of the newest EU members

CHAPTER 4

THE EUROPEAN UNION AND A KNOWLEDGE-BASED SOCIETY

Article 2 of the Treaty on European Union promises, "to promote economic and social progress and a high level of employment." One of the ways the EU has gone about fulfilling this promise is the eEurope initiative. This initiative is based on the belief that getting more European citizens online will create jobs and make European industries more competitive with the rest of the world.

The eEurope initiative was introduced at the November 1999 European Commission. In addition to economic benefits, the initiative was also concerned with educational, government services, health, and cultural entertainment benefits that would come from technology improvements. The eEurope initiative has four component programs: eLearning, eHealth, eGovernment, and eBusiness.

All these programs focus on getting the most use of computer technology for all citizens, not just a privileged few. At the EU March 2000 Summit in Lisbon, the European heads of state set a goal for the EU to be the most competitive knowledge-based society in the world by 2010.

At the time of the Lisbon Summit, only 18 percent of European households had Internet access.

The eEurope initiative has helped connect Europe to the Internet.

The EU is helping to break down barriers between Europe and the rest of the world through the Internet.

By the middle of 2002, the Internet was available to 40 percent of European households. The EU helped achieve this improvement by developing cheaper, faster, and more secure Internet access through encouraging competition. Competitors now challenge national suppliers who once held monopolies on Internet access.

EU countries are not required to make changes in their own laws to achieve the goals, just to share information through the "open coordination method." The EU leaders at the March 2000 Lisbon Summit agreed that in order to fulfill the 1999 eEurope initiative:

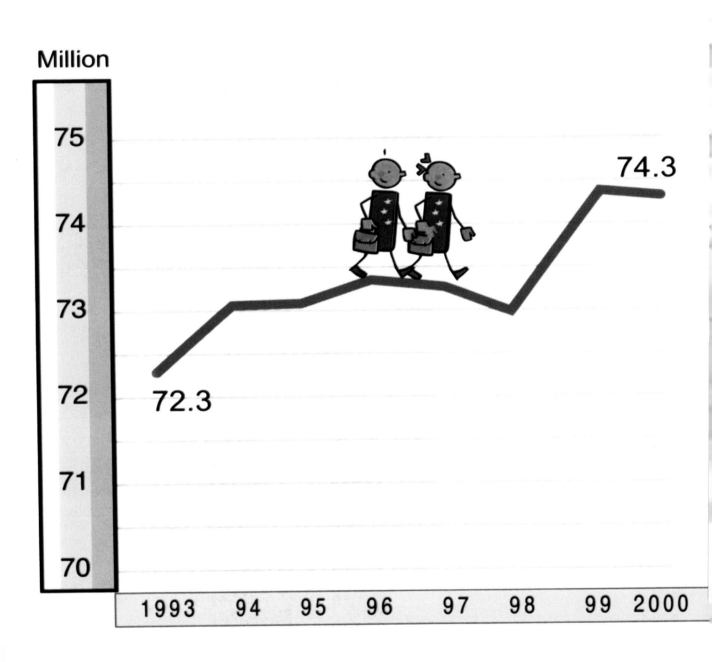

1. businesses and citizens must have access to inexpensive, world-class communications.

2. every citizen must be equipped with skills to live in an information society.

3. a high priority must be given to life-long learning.

By sharing information, and by spending EU budget money on programs to adapt new technologies in poorer regions, progress on the three agreement points has been reached. EU leaders have agreed to keep increasing spending on research so that by 2010, 3 percent of the **gross domestic product** will go toward technology development.

Number of students in millions involved in higher education in the EU between 1993 and 2000

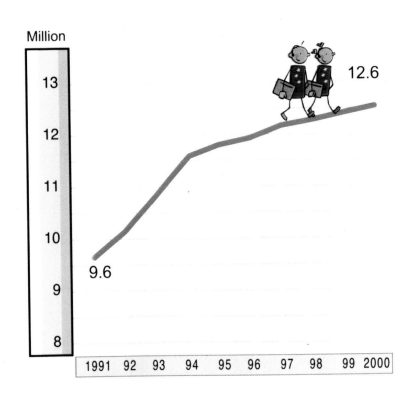

Million

13

12

11

10

9

8

12.6

9.6

1991 92 93 94 95 96 97 98 99 2000

Detailed action plans for the eEurope initiative were created at meetings after the March 2000 Lisbon Summit. A 2002 action plan was set up at the June 2000 Feira Summit. In June 2002, EU leaders in Seville set up a more focused 2005 action plan. The 2005 plan invests more money in research into information and communication technologies.

In 2003, 90 percent of European businesses with more than ten employees had Internet connections, and 60 percent had Web sites. That year, approximately 20 percent of European companies bought and sold over the Internet. Germany and Ireland did the most online business, and Portugal and France the least.

The EU leaders know that Internet access alone is not enough to achieve their goals. The eLearning program is also an important part of the eEurope initiative. The EU finances education programs so that its citizens have computer skills for future jobs and social interaction. The eLearning program coordinates national efforts to modernize education systems. The program aims to link all schools and training centers through the Internet. It also seeks to define a basic European framework of information technology skills, with an ".eu" domain instead of a ".com" for all European citizens, schools, and businesses. The eLearning program achieved a 93 percent Internet access rate for all schools in 2002, up from 89 percent in 2001. In 2001, there was an average of one online computer for every twenty-five students; by 2002, there were seventeen students to every online computer.

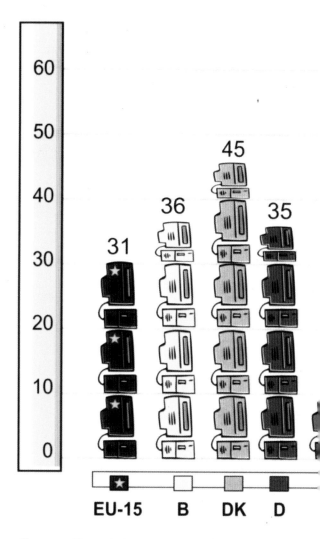

Source: Eurostat

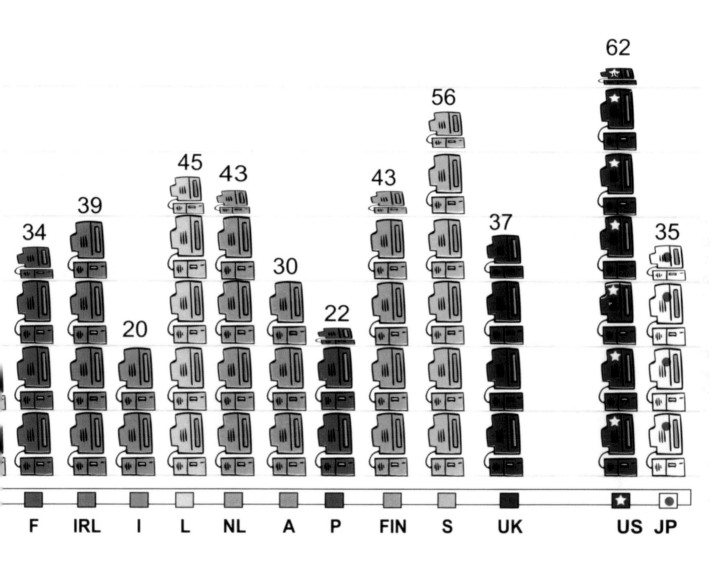

Number of personal computers per 100 people in 2001 in the EU as a whole, as well as the 15 nations that were then members, compared to the United States and Japan

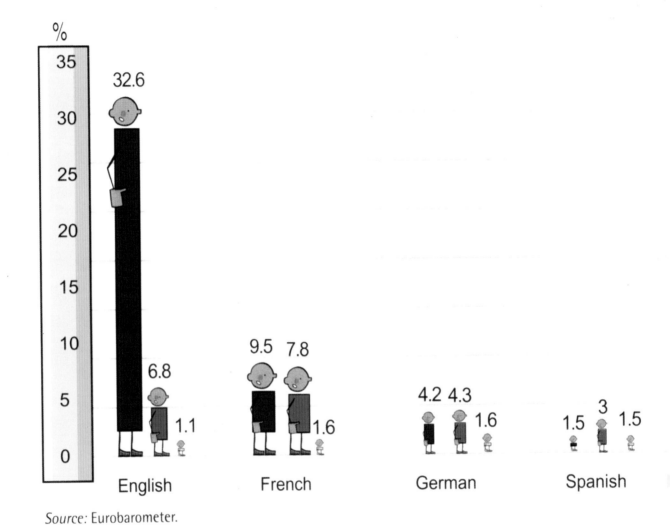

%

35
32.6
30
25
20
15
10
9.5 7.8
5 6.8
4.2 4.3
3
1.1 1.6 1.6 1.5 1.5
0

English   French   German   Spanish

Source: Eurobarometer.

The eLearning program also has an eContent component. The EU recognizes that language barriers keep its citizens from using the Internet. In 2003, 75 percent of all Web sites were in English. The eContent component seeks to increase the use of other languages on the Internet and create sites for all member citizens to use.

With the expected economic growth and trained technology users, the EU hopes to implement its eGovernment and eHealth programs. The eGovernment program will allow citizens to use government services such as these from easy computer access:

1. income taxes

2. job search services

3. social security contributions

4. drivers' licenses

5. car registrations

6. declarations of theft to the police

7. birth and marriage certificates

8. enrollment in universities

9. passport applications

■ First foreign language

■ Second foreign language

□ Third foreign language

1 0.9

ian

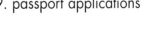

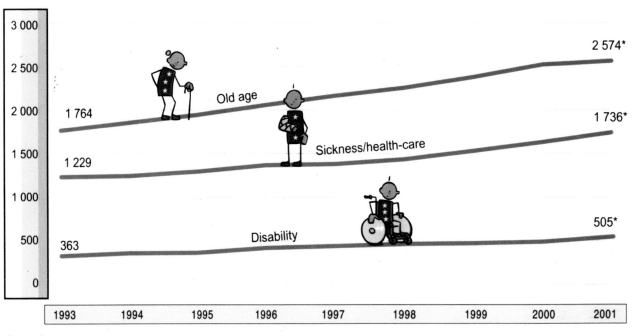

3 000
2 500
2 000
1 500
1 000
500
0

1 764

1 229

363

Old age

Sickness/health-care

Disability

2 574*

1 736*

505*

1993 1994 1995 1996 1997 1998 1999 2000 2001

Source: Eurostat

Spending in the EU between 1993 and 2001 on social benefits per head of household

In April 2002, the European Commission conducted a study that showed 55 percent of basic public services were available online, an increase of 10 percent from October 2001. The study showed that services involving payments to the government were even more readily available, with a 79 percent rate. The eGovernment 2002 study showed that Ireland had the highest score for providing online public services—85 percent. Sweden came in second at 81 percent, with Finland third at 70 percent.

The eHealth program hopes to use computer technology to improve the quality and accessibility of health care, particularly to the disabled. The EU Council of Ministers adopted a resolution in 2002 to help get Internet access to 37 million disabled people by agreeing to a set of internationally recognized standards. The eHealth program also encourages doctors to use the Internet to help all patients. In June 2001, 60 percent of all primary health-care providers were equipped with an Internet connection. This was up from 48 percent in May of 2000. During that time period, the percentage of general practitioner doctors using the Internet to communicate with their patients went up from 12 percent to 34 percent. The European Commission has proposed electronic health cards for member citizens. It also wants to link the computer systems of hospitals and laboratories in member countries. The EU governments have promised to set up Web sites that provide public information on healthy living and illness prevention.

The EU wants to put a "European stamp" on the Internet and overtake the United States in technology growth. It will do this by encouraging multilingual use, training its citizens, increasing access, and creating more European online systems. Its plan is to improve the lives of its citizens by increasing jobs and improving government services and health care. The statistics show that the plans are working.

Estonia, one of the EU's newest members, will benefit from the EU's economic support.

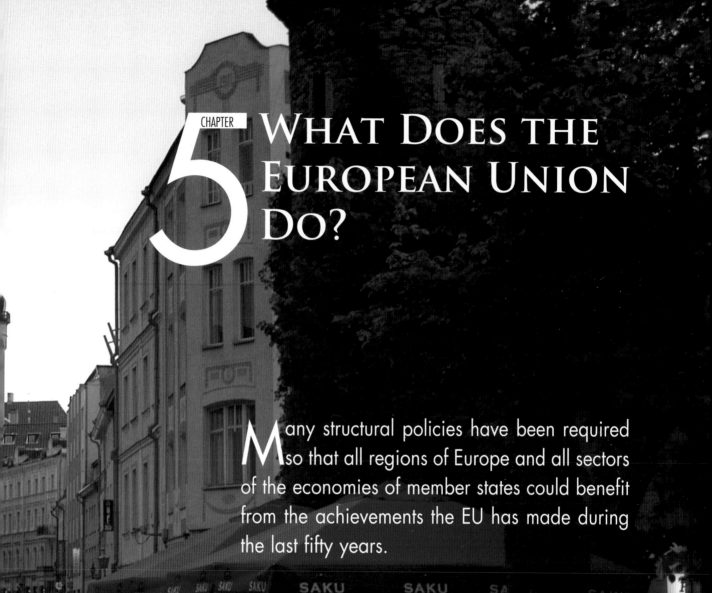

5 WHAT DOES THE EUROPEAN UNION DO?

Many structural policies have been required so that all regions of Europe and all sectors of the economies of member states could benefit from the achievements the EU has made during the last fifty years.

For example, many regional and social policies have been introduced to narrow the economic gap between richer and poorer regions. The EU's regional policies allow its budget to help its poorer members. Two hundred thirteen billion euros have been promised to such regions for the years 2000 through 2006. These payments will go to modernize farming, help people find jobs, and convert old industries into modern, economically profitable ones.

The EU use three criteria to determine member state eligibility for this money:

1. when the gross domestic product of a member state is less than 75 percent of the EU average.

2. when certain areas are being restructured, are declining, or are in economic crisis.

3. when job training for workers is needed.

Specific programs to achieve these goals are the "Interre," promoting cooperation across borders, and "Irban," which works with cities in crisis.

The EU has many parts that all work together.

15

Europe is proud of its "bright idea," a union with economic and political power.

Structures within the EU have been expanded even further to accommodate the ten new member states introduced in 2004. The "Phare" program will channel 10.9 billion euros to candidate countries in central and Eastern Europe between the years 2000 and 2006. The ISPA (Instrument for Structural Policies for Pre-Accession) will provide 7.2 billion euros for environmental and transportation projects. "Sapard" has a budget of 3.6 billion euros for agriculture.

The EU also seeks to correct social inequalities. The European Social Fund (ESF) was set up in 1961 to create jobs and to help workers switch careers. In 2003, the ESF's budget was 4.8 billion euros.

Social progress is also supported by EU laws, which protect workers' health and ensure their fair wages. In 1991, the Maastricht European Council established the Community Charter of Basic Social Rights. These rights included free movement of citizens, fair pay, and improved working conditions.

Until 1997, more than 10 percent of Europe's workforce was unemployed. At the European Council in Luxembourg on November 20 and 21, 1997, the fifteen member states agreed on new strategies for better job training, starting new businesses, and improving dialogues between employers and employees. These goals are referred to as the "Luxembourg Strategy," and have been increased by the European Council in Lisbon in March 2000. These same policies then became known as the "Lisbon Strategy," with the new goal of making the EU

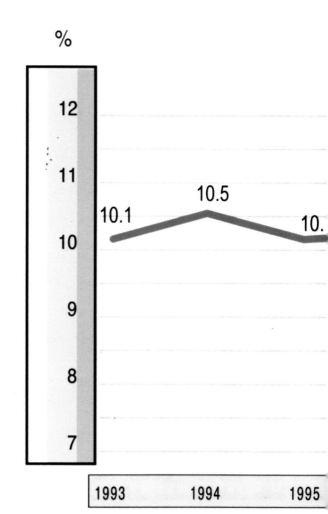

Source: Eurostat

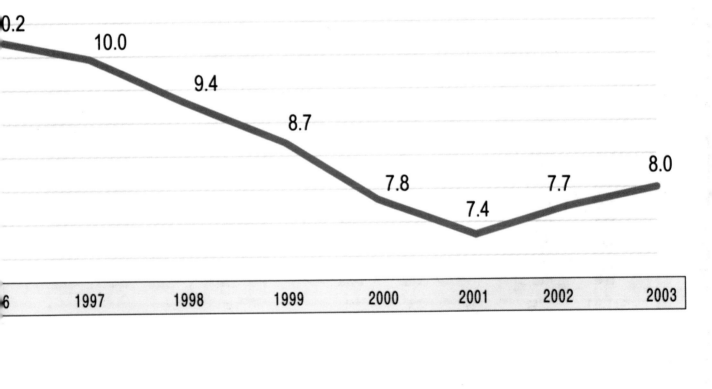

0.2

10.0

9.4

8.7

7.8

7.4

7.7

8.0

6   1997   1998   1999   2000   2001   2002   2003

The EU believes that it can use its power to act as a "lighthouse" for the rest of the world.

"the most competitive and dynamic knowledge-based economy in the world" within ten years.

In March 1999, the Berlin European Council agreed on "Agenda 2000," a plan to make certain the EU has enough money to implement its policies through the year 2006. Agenda 2000 also aims at disciplining the EU members to live within their established budgets. Agenda 2000 has led to some successful results. For example, the EU's budget for 2003 was well below its ceiling at 100 billion euros.

The Berlin Summit also reformed EU's agriculture policy to keep its farming industry competitive. Even though early EU policies had helped agriculture grow, the farming community had shrunk from 20 percent of the population to less than 5 percent. In 2002, to aid farming, the EU gave 45.4 billion euros to subsidize agriculture, 40 percent of its entire budget.

One of Agenda 2000's aims was to encourage farmers to pro- duce quality products rather than great quantities of products—a change from a previous policy that had resulted in surpluses. Farmers are also encouraged by Agenda 2000 to use more environmentally friendly methods.

Finally, the 2002 Commission proposed reforms that would prevent a recurrence of the spread of mad cow disease and foot and mouth disease, which had spread across Europe in the 1990s and early 2000s.

EU policies have grown from their economic emphases to address environmental concerns, health, consumer rights, transportation, and education. Since most of these are cross-border issues, EU legislation is needed to resolve them. For example, because pollution knows no geographic boundaries, the EU has adopted air pollution standards protecting the ozone layer by reducing emissions of chlorofluorocarbons (CFCs). The EU has also set new policies to conserve and manage natural resources alongside their goal of boosting Europe's technological capacity.

In 1958, the European Community had set up the European Atomic Energy Community in order to remain world leaders in technology and to exploit nuclear power for peaceful purposes. Since then, with new scientific innovations, European research has had to diversify. In June 2002, the EU had a budget of 17.5 billion euros to finance a series of projects that would bring together thousands of researchers from all over the EU.

The EU flag

6 CHAPTER THE EUROPEAN UNION, FREEDOM, SECURITY, AND JUSTICE

Even though the EU tries to guarantee its citizens freedom from violence, crime, and terrorism, these problems remain major concerns for Europeans. Because of the single-market economy, such challenges must be met by the entire union, rather than by individual governments. And with its recent enlargement to twenty-five member states, the EU has been pushed to confront these matters swiftly.

The original Treaty of Rome of 1957 never addressed issues like crime. Only later did the freedom of movement of EU's citizens make it clear that all Europeans must have the same access to justice. Therefore, later amendments to the Treaty of Rome have begun to address the protection of EU's citizens. These amendments have included the Single European Act, and the Treaties of Maastricht and Amsterdam. Specific policies have included a stronger emphasis on the EU's external borders, since checkpoints have slowly been abolished on borders between various European nations. Also, police forces and judicial authorities from all European countries have begun to work together to combat crime.

On October 15 and 16, 1999, the European Council called a special meeting at Tampere, Finland, to discuss issues of freedom, security, and justice in the EU. Some sixty steps were to be taken before 2004 to protect Europe's citizens, with the European Commission being given the task of monitoring the implementation of these steps. Below are some of the steps that were proposed during this meeting:

1. establishment of a common EU policy on **asylum** and immigration

2. establishment of a genuine "European area of justice"

3. an EU-wide fight against crime

4. stronger external action

With these goals in mind, the EU remains aware that policies for justice within the EU must be carefully balanced with policies for freedom. For example, in 1985, Belgium, France, Germany, Luxembourg, and the Netherlands agreed to abolish all checks on persons at the borders between their countries. This agreement, known as the Schengen Agreement, required EU citizens to present only an identity card or a passport when traveling. Since March 2001, Iceland, Norway, Austria, Denmark, Finland, Greece, Italy, Portugal, Spain, and Sweden have also implemented the Schengen Agreement.

Besides the possible spreading of criminal activity, the rising number of immigrants is a problem associated with the EU's lack of internal borders. The council's meeting at Tampere established common asylum procedures for all EU nations. Also, immigrants are to be judged by the same set of rules within all countries of the EU.

One immigration problem has been the activity of criminal gangs who run people-smuggling networks and exploit vulnerable human beings, especially women and children. These criminals have become very sophisticated within the last ten years and have learned to use European networks for their activities. Organized crime and terrorism have also become more brutal and clever across the globe within the last decade; they are among the EU's growing concerns.

To combat such crime, the Schengen Information System (SIS) is a complex database to exchange information between countries. It allows

The EU helps organize the various laws of its member nations.

law enforcement to exchange information on wanted people and property—for example, stolen vehicles or works of art, or persons for whom an arrest warrant or **extradition request** has been issued. Another way to catch criminals is to track the money received from criminal activity. To this end, the EU has passed laws to stop money laundering.

The greatest advance in security within the EU is Europol, a group of police and customs officers that services the entire union. Europol addresses such issues as drug trafficking, stolen vehicles, people smuggling, sexual exploitation of women and children, pornography, forgery, the selling of

Working toward a more stable EU

CHAPTER SIX—THE EUROPEAN UNION: FREEDOM, SECURITY, AND JUSTICE 69

The EU legal system provides for an appeals process.

nuclear materials, terrorism, money laundering, and counterfeiting the euro.

Unfortunately, fifteen different judicial systems within the EU enforce laws in ways that confuse many who continually travel from one European country to another. Several EU programs have been set up to bring together law professionals from different member states. The Grotius Program helps lawyers and judges learn how legal systems in other European countries work. The Falcone Program develops contacts between judges, prosecution services, and police forces. And Eurojust enables investigators from various countries to work together to solve crimes.

> The Grotius Programs help educate lawyers and judges throughout the EU, so that they can better understand each other's legal systems.

Finally, cooperation between courts in various countries can be hurt by differing definitions of criminal acts, as well as by sentencing variations. To deal effectively with these concerns, the EU is compiling a common **penal** policy, as well as a common legal framework for fighting terrorism.

Until 1997, immigration and judicial cooperation for law enforcement were matters that required cooperation between the various EU governments. However, the Treaty of Amsterdam transferred these issues to the "community" domain. This move took place, however, during a five-year transitional period, wherein decisions were shared between the European Commission and the member states of the EU. The EU's goals, however, are clear: an enforceable system throughout all member nations, ensuring its citizens' safety and security.

France is one of the EU's founding members.

7 THE EUROPEAN UNION AND THE FUTURE

In 1849, the writer Victor Hugo predicted that "a day will come when all the nations of this continent, without losing their distinct qualities of their glorious individuality, will fuse together and form the European Brotherhood." It took more than one hundred years for Hugo's dream to even begin, in the form of the EU. And even now, after another fifty years, new challenges and difficulties are still being presented.

In 2004, the EU enlarged to twenty-five member states, with further enlargement predicted during the period between 2007 and 2015. After this goal has been reached, leaders must then decide whether to draw final geographical boundaries around the EU.

Even during such times of change, the half billion people of the EU still agree on a "foundational agreement," an agreement that continues to emphasize the traditional European values of peace, security, democracy, and justice—with each of the EU's member states sharing some of its power to achieve these aims.

Today's technological revolution presents economic challenges, as well as risks such as spilled oil tankers or Chernobyl-type nuclear accidents. National policies alone can't secure the economic growth of European countries. To hope to combat these problems, the EU must act as a single force.

The EU is also affected by upheavals in other parts of the world, such as the renewal of religious fervor in the Islamic world, starvation in Africa, unilateral tendencies in North America, overcrowding in Asia, or the global shifting of businesses and careers. Because of these concerns, the EU must continue to be involved in the world's development, as well as that of its member states.

Europe must adjust to the growing number of challenges in today's world. Each new member state adds a new force that threatens to break apart the union. Countries often have short-term policies that threaten the long-term goals of the

Malta, one of the EU's newest members.

The EU is a thriving community.

EU as a whole. Only a democratic political system with checks and balances will allow so many various cultures to remain distinct while also working toward a single goal.

The constitution of the EU has been designed to simplify the policies within the treaties and to clearly explain the government's decision-making process. One purpose of this constitution is to explain the goals and ideals of the EU so that its citizens will be motivated to become part of its democratic process. Within the constitution, both the will of the people and the legitimacy of their national governments are supported.

It is still too early to know whether the constitution is the final project that completes the EU, or whether the political structures in Europe will evolve even further. In 2005, member states are voting to **ratify** the constitution. In early results, most of the member states have defeated the constitution. Regardless of whether or not the constitution is approved, one thing is certain: the EU is a growing political and economic force on the twenty-first century's world stage.

PROJECT AND REPORT IDEAS

Map

- Make a map of Europe and color code the members of the EU based on the year they joined.

Reports

- Write a report describing how the EU has changed since its creation.
- Write a report describing how a country is admitted into the EU.
- Imagine you live in a country that has joined the EU. Write a description about how your country has changed since becoming a member state.

Projects

- Imagine you represent a country asking for admission to the EU. Present to the class your argument for admission.
- Read more about the proposed EU constitution, and stage a debate with one side in favor of ratifying the constitution and one side against.
- Make a poster of the phrase "Hello" in the languages of all of the EU member states.
- Hold a Europe Day celebration.

CHRONOLOGY

1914	World War I begins; it ends in 1918.
1939	World War II begins; it ends in 1945.
1951	Treaty of Paris creates the European Coal and Steel Community.
1957	Treaty of Rome establishes the European Economic Community (EEC).
1958	The European Atomic Energy Community is established.
1961	European Social Fund is established.
July 1, 1968	All customs duties are removed for members of the EEC.
1973	Denmark, Ireland, and the United Kingdom join the EEC.
1975	The European Regional Development Fund is established.
1979	The European monetary system begins.
1981	Greece joins the EEC.
1986	Spain and Portugal join the EEC.
July 1987	Single European Act is established.
1990	Communism falls in Europe.
1991	Community Charter of Basic Social Rights is established.
December 1991	The Treaty on European Union creates the European Union as known today; it is officially recognized on November 1, 1993.
1994	European Monetary Institute is established.
January 1, 1995	Austria, Finland, and Sweden join the EU.
October 2, 1997	Treaty of Amsterdam is signed, becomes effective May 1, 1999.
1998	European National Bank is established.
November 1999	eEurope Initiative is introduced.
March 2000	The Lisbon Strategy is adopted.
February 26, 2001	Treaty of Nice is signed; becomes effective February 1, 2003.
January 1, 2002	The euro goes into circulation.
January 2003	European Union Police Mission begins operations in Bosnia and Herzegovina.
2004	European Union expands to twenty-five members.

FURTHER READING/INTERNET RESOURCES

Beach, Derek. *The Dynamics of European Integration: Why and When EU Institutions Matter.* New York: Palgrave Macmillan, 2005.

Dunnan, Nancy. *One Europe.* Boston, Mass.: Houghton Mifflin, 1992.

Jones, M. A. *The European Union: How Does It Work?* Oxford, U.K.: Oxford University Press, 2003.

McCormick, John. *Environmental Policy in the European Union.* New York: Palgrave Macmillan, 2001.

McCormick, John. *Understanding the European Union: A Concise Introduction.* New York: Palgrave Macmillan, 2002.

Pusca, Anca. *European Union: Challenges and Promises of a New Enlargement.* New York: International Debate Education Association, 2004.

Europa—The European Union Online
europa.eu.int/

European Union in the United States
www.eurunion.org

European Union Institute for Security Studies
www.iss-eu.org

European Union Parliament
www.europarl.europa.eu/

European Union Studies Association
www.eustudies.org

European Union at the United Nations
www.europa-eu-un.org

Publisher's note:
The Web sites listed on this page were active at the time of publication. The publisher is not responsible for Web sites that have changed their addresses or discontinued operation since the date of publication. The publisher will review and update the Web-site list upon each reprint.

FOR MORE INFORMATION

Delegation of the European Commission to the United States
2300 M Street NW
Washington DC 20037
Tel.: 202-862-9500
Fax: 202-429-1766

European Commission
222 East 41st Street
Floors 21 and 22
New York, NY 10017
Tel.: 212-371-3804
Fax: 212-238-5191
e-mail: Delegation-New-York-EUInfo@cec.eu.int

European Parliament
Rue Wiertz
B.P. 1047
B-1047 Brussels, Belgium
Tel.: 32-2-284-2111
Fax: 32-2-284-9075

U.S. Mission to the European Union
13 Zinnerstraat
B-1000 Brussels, Belgium
Tel.: 32-2-508-2222
Fax: 32-2-512-5720

assent: To agree to something.

asylum: A place of refuge and protection.

auditors: Someone who is qualified to examine the accounts of a business or organization.

censure: To express official disapproval or condemnation.

co-decision: A decision made in agreement with more than one person.

common market: An economic association established between nations with the aim of eliminating or reducing trade barriers.

consultation: A discussion aimed at ascertaining opinions or reaching an agreement.

conventions: Agreements between groups, especially international agreements, that are slightly less formal than treaties.

deficit: The amount by which expenses exceed income.

democratization: The act of taking steps toward the establishment of a democracy.

deployed: Put into action.

extradition request: A request by one jurisdiction to another to have a criminal or suspect returned to that jurisdiction for a legal proceeding.

federation: A political unit formed from smaller units who defer certain powers to a central government while retaining some measure of self-government.

gross domestic product: The total monetary amount of all goods and services produced within a country in a year, minus the net income from investments in other countries.

inflation: An increase in the supply of currency or credit without a corresponding increase in the availability of goods and services to purchase.

information society: A society characterized by widespread electronic access to information through the use of computers.

intermediary: Someone who acts as a go-between to try and bring about an agreement.

legislative: Involved in the writing and passing of laws.

maladministration: Incompetent or dishonest management or administration, especially in public affairs.

market economies: Economies in which prices and wages are determined mainly by the market and the laws of supply and demand, and not through government regulations.

mediates: Works with all sides in a dispute in an attempt to help them reach an agreement.

monopolies: Companies that control an industry or are the only providers of a product or service.

penal: Relating to, forming, or prescribing punishment by the law.

ratify: To officially approve.

service industries: Businesses that provide a service rather than products.

standardized: Removed variations and brought all types or examples of something into conformity.

Index

PICTURE CREDITS

BIOGRAPHIES

AUTHOR

Having grown up on a farm in southern Virginia, James Stafford now lives on the Southern Tier of New York State with his wife and daughter. He teaches writing and literature at Elmira College.

SERIES CONSULTANTS

Ambassador John Bruton served as Irish Prime Minister from 1994 until 1997. As prime minister, he helped turn Ireland's economy into one of the fastest-growing in the world. He was also involved in the Northern Ireland Peace Process, which led to the 1998 Good Friday Agreement. During his tenure as Ireland's prime minister, he also presided over the European Union presidency in 1996 and helped finalize the Stability and Growth Pact, which governs management of the euro. Before being named the European Commission Head of Delegation in the United States, he was a member of the convention that drafted the European Constitution, signed October 29, 2004.

The European Commission Delegation to the United States represents the interests of the European Union as a whole, much as ambassadors represent their countries' interests to the U.S. government. Matters coming under European Commission authority are negotiated between the commission and the U.S. administration.